How? What? Why?

Why does it fall over?

Jim Pipe

Copper Beech Books
Brookfield • Connecticut

Why do you fall over?

Jo, Zack, and Steve are playing out in the yard. Jo wants to try out her new skates. Zack and Steve have skated before, so they help her learn. But it is not easy!

When Jo tries to skate on one foot, she soon starts to wobble!

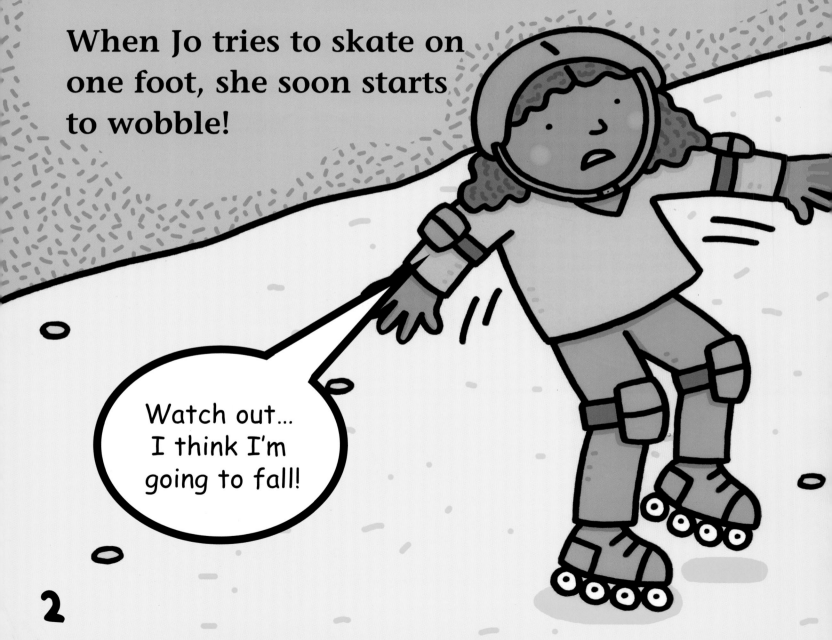

Watch out... I think I'm going to fall!

Let's see how the children find out.

I can't push Steve over when he is spread out like this.

3

Why it works

Things that are wide at the bottom are more steady. If you stand on one foot, you soon start to wobble. But it is easy to keep steady on two feet, and even easier if you spread your feet out. On your hands and knees you spread out even more, so you are very steady.

Solve the puzzle!

Why is a bicycle harder to ride than a tricycle? Think about how wide they are at the bottom.

Why does it fall over?

The children go inside to play. "Let's see who can build the tallest tower," says Zack's mom.

Zack and Jo make their towers the same size all the way up. But Steve puts a big, heavy block on top and his tower falls over!

Oops! I think my tower is too heavy.

7

But a big lump of clay at the top makes it very easy to tip over!

So the heavy block at the top made Steve's tower fall over.

Why it works

Things balance best if most of their weight is at the bottom. If something is heavy at the top, it is much easier to tip over. Things also tip over if too much weight is on one side. Steve's tower also fell over because the block at the top wasn't on straight.

Solve the puzzle

Do some things never fall over? Ask an adult to cut a table tennis ball in half, and fill one half with clay. Stick a straw into the middle of the clay. What happens when you tip the straw over?

3

9

How can three people sit on a seesaw?

The children go outside to play. Steve sits on one end of the seesaw. But when Jo and Zack get on the other end, Steve goes whizzing up into the air!

It's no good. We are much heavier than Steve.

I think one of us needs to get off.

11

Let's see how the children find out.

When I move the two coins nearer the middle it balances! So Jo and I need to sit nearer the middle of the seesaw, too.

3

Why it works

Everything has a point where it balances. On a seesaw this point is in the middle. The farther away from this point you sit, the more you make the seesaw tip. So one person at the end balances two people sitting nearer the middle.

Solve the puzzle

Can you balance three coins against one? Make your own seesaw with a ruler and a pencil, and try.

What keeps a crane from toppling over?

Later on, Zack's friend Amy comes over to his house. Her mom is taking all the children to the circus! On the way, Zack sees a tall crane lifting a heavy pipe.

Won't that heavy pipe make the crane fall over?

It's okay. I'm sure the crane is wide at the bottom.

16

But if we put a wooden block on the other end it balances the marbles in the cup.

3

So the weight on the other end of the crane keeps it from falling over, too.

Why it works

Do you remember how two people balance a seesaw by sitting at either end? Jo's wooden block balances the weight of the marbles in the same way.

On a real crane, heavy weights balance the crane when it lifts something heavy.

Solve the puzzle

Can you make a pencil cup balance? What happens when you put all the pencils on one side? Think about how a crane balances.

How does she balance?

Before the show starts, it is very dark. Then a light comes on. Everyone looks up. High above them, a woman is walking along a tightrope.

How does she do it? The wire is so thin.

I think putting her arms out helps her balance.

That's amazing! The forks make the potato balance on its end.

3

So the pole did help the woman on the tightrope!

Why it works

Things that are heavier at the bottom balance well. The pole adds weight low down, so it helps the woman balance. The forks add weight below the potato, so they make it balance very well. If the woman tips to one side, she can also move the pole quickly the other way to balance herself. If you put your arms out they can balance you in the same way.

Solve the puzzle

How do birds balance on a thin wire? Think about long parts on their body that may help them.

21

Did you solve the puzzles?

Why is a bicycle harder to ride than a tricycle?

A bicycle is hard to balance when you ride slowly, because it has only two narrow wheels. The three wheels on a tricycle make it much wider at the bottom, so it is much more steady. When Steve spread himself out on page 5, he was very steady too.

Do some things never fall over?

Things that are heavy at the bottom are hard to tip over, like the bottle on page 8.

With the table tennis ball, the clay is much heavier than the straw, so the weight is all at the bottom. When you tip the straw, it wobbles, but it doesn't fall over!

Can you balance three coins with one?

On page 13, Zack got two coins nearer the middle to balance with one farther out. If you move the three coins even closer to the middle, they will also balance with a single coin.

How do you make a pencil cup balance?

If you put the pencils all on one side, the pencil cup falls over. But if you put them opposite each other, they balance, like the pipe and the weights on the crane.

How do birds sit on a thin wire?

On page 19, the woman balances on the tightrope with a long pole. A bird balances on a thin wire by using its tail like the pole.

Index

© Aladdin Books Ltd 2002

Designed and produced by
Aladdin Books Ltd
28 Percy Street
London W1T 2BZ

First published in
the United States in 2002 by
Copper Beech Books,
an imprint of
The Millbrook Press
2 Old New Milford Road
Brookfield, Connecticut 06804

ISBN 0-7613-2721-5 (Library bdg.)

ISBN 0-7613-1686-8 (Trade h'cover)

Cataloging-in-Publication data is
is on file at the Library of Congress.

Printed in U.A.E.
All rights reserved

Literacy Consultant
Jackie Holderness
Westminster Institute of Education,
Oxford Brookes University, England

Science Consultant
Michael Brown

Science Testers
Ben, Toby, and Elliott Fussell

Design
Flick, Book Design and Graphics

Illustration
Jo Moore

For Chloé Guerif